The Introverted Educator

In today's world of education, teachers face increasing pressure to design classrooms with high engagement and larger-than-life atmospheres. But how do you make that work if you or your students are introverts and more reticent to speak up? This unique book has the secrets to creating a *Dead Poets Society* classroom even if you're not quite a Robin Williams!

The book offers insights on effective instruction through the eyes of six dynamic and effective, yet introverted, educators. The teachers share their experiences and strategies for how they brought magic into their instruction and made their classrooms come to life for students. Their inspiring real-life stories demonstrate that there is no one right way to teach – if you don't want to jump on a table in a costume, you can reach and engage students in your own unique way!

Appropriate for teachers of all subject areas, the book also offers research-backed ways to recognize and support the students who are not the "talkers" or the first ones to volunteer. It also includes book reflection questions so teachers and administrators can better support introverted educators and students alike.

Dr. Rochelle Green is an introvert and 15-year veteran educator with a passion to reach all students through instruction that supports how they learn best. Rochelle currently teaches and supervises elementary education for University of Wyoming – Casper and is the director for Bachelor of Applied Science Program in Organizational Leadership.

Also Available from Routledge
Eye on Education
(www.routledge.com/k-12)

**Group Work that Works: Student Collaboration for
21st Century Success**
Paul J. Vermette and Cynthia L. Kline

**Beyond Think-Pair-Share: A Quick Guide to
Effective Collaboration**
Christina M. Krantz and Laura Gullette Smith

**Joyful Learning: Infusing Your 6–12 Classroom with
Meaning, Relevance, and Fun**
Stephanie Farley

**Passionate Learners, 3e: How to Engage and
Empower Your Students**
Pernille Ripp

**Empowering Students for the Future: Using the Right
Questions to Teach the Value of Passion, Success, and Failure**
Eric Yuhasz

The Introverted Educator

Redefining Participation and Creating
Quiet Magic in the Classroom

Rochelle Green

Routledge
Taylor & Francis Group

NEW YORK AND LONDON

Designed cover image: © Jane Khomi / Getty Images

First published 2023
by Routledge
605 Third Avenue, New York, NY 10158

and by Routledge
4 Park Square, Milton Park, Abingdon, Oxon, OX14 4RN

Routledge is an imprint of the Taylor & Francis Group, an informa business

Library of Congress Cataloging-in-Publication Data
Names: Green, Rochelle M., author.
Title: The introverted educator : redefining participation and creating quiet magic in the classroom / Rochelle Green.
Description: New York : Routledge, 2023. | Includes bibliographical references.
Identifiers: LCCN 2022057029 (print) | LCCN 2022057030 (ebook) | ISBN 9781032341477 (Hardback) | ISBN 9781032340623 (Paperback) | ISBN 9781003321750 (eBook)
Subjects: LCSH: Communication in education. | Teacher-student relationships—Case studies. | Introverts. | Introversion in children. | Bashfulness in children. | Self-confidence in children.
Classification: LCC LB1033.5 .G74 2023 (print) | LCC LB1033.5 (ebook) | DDC 371.102/2—dc23/eng/20230120
LC record available at https://lccn.loc.gov/2022057029
LC ebook record available at https://lccn.loc.gov/2022057030

ISBN: 978-1-032-34147-7 (hbk)
ISBN: 978-1-032-34062-3 (pbk)
ISBN: 978-1-003-32175-0 (ebk)

DOI: 10.4324/9781003321750

Typeset in Palatino
by Apex CoVantage, LLC

This book is dedicated to all the brave introverts, and all educators, who have believed in themselves and knew they could make a difference in the life of a child.

Contents

Acknowledgments

I would like to acknowledge all the people who have supported me in this author journey. Dr. Cindy Brock, you were my inspiration to take the first step and put my dream into action. Dr. Brent Pickett, thank you for believing in me. Without my loving husband, Thomas James, by my side to share this dream, it would mean nothing. I could not have done this without the support of my loving and amazing family.

Meet the author

Dr. Rochelle Green is an introvert and 15-year veteran educator with a passion to reach all students through instruction that supports how they learn best. Rochelle currently teaches and supervises elementary education for University of Wyoming – Casper and is the director for Bachelor of Applied Science Organizational Leadership. Prior to going into education, she served in the United States Air Force for nine years, traveling all over the world.  The loves of her life are her amazing, supportive husband, Tom, and three independent and incredible sons, Logan, Joseph, and Anthony. Family, including her furry family members, means everything to her!

Introduction

It had been just like any ordinary school day in the life of an educator. I had finished my day of teaching a group of amazing students and was waiting in a classroom for our weekly staff meeting. Glancing around the room, I was met with exhausted faces, ones that read the look of wanting to get this meeting over with and go home. Our principal made his entrance into the room. This was no ordinary entrance. As he made his way across the room, he leapt up on a table and drew his imaginary sword. This gained him well-deserved laughs as well as a few pretend screams.

The focus of this day's staff meeting was student engagement, excitement, and going beyond typical instruction to reach students as they had never been before. As I once again glanced around the room, I observed mixed reactions. A handful of my fellow educators were ready to jump up on a table with him; these teachers were enjoying the excitement he brought to the room. Then I observed numerous educators almost shrinking in their chairs as if trying to disappear. Their expressions screamed, "Please don't call on me" and "Is it time to go home yet?"

It was then and there that I reflected on the simple fact that not all teachers are the same. Every one of us enters the profession with different ideas, personalities, and passions. Each of us engages students in our own way. Some of us are outgoing, ready to run through the room jumping on tables and drawing our swords in an effort to engage our students. Some of us are

DOI: 10.4324/9781003321750-1

quiet, reflective, and ready to reach students in different, yet effective ways. As we were exiting the classroom, a book title popped in my head, *The Dead Poets Society Classroom for the Not-So-Robin-Williams*. This one experience and moment became the premise, inspiration, and passion for this book.

It is estimated that 16% to 50% of our population is made up of introverts (Houston, 2019; Myers, 2019). In any given classroom, up to 10 students could have introverted tendencies (Education World). In today's world of education, teachers are stressed by the increasing demands of providing a classroom with high engagement and larger-than-life atmospheres. However, introverts, both educators and students alike, often find energy within themselves and not from external activities (Silverman, 1993).

This book will give insight into effective instruction in elementary through secondary classrooms through the eyes of six dynamic and effective, yet introverted, educators. The six focus teachers inside this book will share their stories and strategies for how they brought magic into their instruction and made their classrooms come to life for their students.

Through real-life stories and experiences from K–12 educators, involving humor, challenges, success stories, and suggestions for fellow teachers, those educating our future will gain insight into how to understand students and educators who are introverted in nature. The suggestions will include not only ideas for teaching but also for helping educate and reach students who are introverted. Through personal experiences, these educators will share what has worked for them. If you're an introverted educator, you'll see that you're not alone, that there are other effective educators who are successfully reaching and engaging students in their own unique ways.

What I hope you will get out of the book:

♦ real-life K–12 teacher experiences from the perspective of introverts;
♦ strategies for reaching introverted students;
♦ suggestions for creating an atmosphere that benefits all students, both extroverted and introverted;

◆ research that supports a variety of methods to educate introverted students;
◆ supporting research and book reflection questions to aid educators and administrators move toward effective strategies for this population of students;
◆ implications for educators' conclusion chapter;
◆ implications for where do we go from here?

Throughout the next few chapters, you will experience real-life stories of introverts who have journeyed into education and have created quiet magic for their students every day.

Meet Zach

An introverted educator who finds magic teaching theater

I have spent a great deal of my life in front of people. I am a father, a husband, a theater teacher, and an arts advocate. I have dedicated my life to helping introverts come out and extroverts stay out!

Tell me about your journey that brought you to education. How did being more introverted impact this journey?

What brought me to education? I always loved school. I learned to read before I was in kindergarten. I always loved books, and that's where my nose was. And so, when I started school, I was really excited about it. I did really well. When the school district was starting up the gifted and talented (G.T.) program in the '80s, I was one of the kids that they started doing what they called "enrichment programming" for.

As elementary school went on and kids started growing up and getting into that social stratification, I went to a school with a very large . . . well, first of all, it was a very high-socioeconomic population, with a lot of white-collar students, and my dad wasn't. He owned a sewer cleaning company. Some of the

DOI: 10.4324/9781003321750-2

socioeconomic differences started to come out in about 3rd, 4th grade but so did differences in things we were interested in. Most of my male peers gravitated toward sports, and it was just not something I was gifted in. I tried soccer and really didn't do well. I tried T-ball and didn't do well. Well, I was more geared toward the arts. I joined the children's chorale when I was in 5th grade mostly because I wanted to go to New York City, not because I thought, "Oh, I want to perform." Although, there were times in school where performing interested me.

But because of that, not being into sports and being more into alternative music and ways of dressing and things, I got made fun of a lot in about 4th or 5th grade. And I think that's where my introvert tendencies were planted – in those peer relationships where I was being bullied or made fun of because I wasn't into the sports aspect or I wasn't part of the same socioeconomic group. I think that's where a lot of my self-doubt came in. And I think that's where a lot of people will say, "Well, you are a performer, you've done theater." I mean, I've been on stages in New York. I've been to stages Wyoming and in Colorado. But what I found is that when I hang around a lot of other "theater people," they're always on. There's always this performative aspect to them, and they're like, "I'm here and I'm out." And I never was that way. When I was in children's chorale, my parents would say, "Sing for us, sing for us," to put me on the spot. And I just thought, "Nope. Nope. Don't want to do that. Nope," which is an odd thing.

And so, I went through school, and I did a lot of outgoing things. If you looked at me on the outside, you would say, "Yeah, he's a pretty extroverted guy." I did theater. I did speeches and debates. I was the editor of the school paper. I was elected the student body president. I mean, I did a lot of things, and I put myself out there a lot.

Getting up in front of a big group of people, while it takes a lot of self-encouragement to do it, it's really natural and comfortable for me. What isn't is the small-group social stuff. If I go to a party and I don't know that many people, I hit the corner.

I really enjoyed school. And then, after I got out of elementary school and was able to get into middle school and high school, that social thing didn't matter as much because there were more people and more social groups to be a part of. Although I did all of these things in high school, I never really felt like I was in any of the groups. I loved being in the clubs, but I never felt like I was part of the group. I kind of felt like I was this outside person that would then do it, and then I would move back outside that circle.

Before going into teaching, I became a reporter and one thing that I found that was really difficult was to do the face-to-face, assertive kind of questioning. Telephones? I love the telephone. I called people up all the time and that was usually the way I accommodated that stage fright that I would feel when I would go into situations where it was smaller-group, in-person things. Which, I mean, that was interesting because it was the first time, I really felt like . . . It felt like I'm an extrovert that progressed to introversion, but I still love getting up in front of crowds, and I still love . . . But for me, now, it's more as a director than it is as the actor, which I think fits me a lot better.

While I was a reporter, I covered education. So, I got to go into a lot of schools, and I got to see what teachers were doing and what was going on in schools. When I realized that the journalism thing wasn't going to allow me to really get ahead . . . I was making, I don't know, like $20,000 a year. It was untenable. And so, I decided then I was going to go back to school and get my teaching certification. Then I met my current wife, we got married, and things are a lot better in that regard.

I taught a year of 8th grade language arts, and it was not the right fit for me. I made connections with students, but it just didn't feel like I was connecting. I got a call from a principal, who said, "The theater job at the high school is open. You should apply for it." And I said, "Well, I don't have the certification for that. I never . . ." And he said, "Don't worry about it. You'll be fine. You'll be perfect." I sat on it until the very last day that applications were due. I woke up at like 3:00 in the morning, and I turned over to my wife and woke her up. I said, "I'm going to apply for that job." She goes, "What took you so long?"

So, I did, and I ended up getting it. I absolutely love it. But what I find is . . . while it's easy for me to get up in front of a crowd of people and tell them to turn their cell phones off and introduce the great things that my kids are doing, I have a harder time . . . I remember the first theater conference I went to, the National Theater Conference, and I didn't know anybody. I realized that what I do is, if I'm in large things like that, again, I'm outside that circle and kind of just observe. Really, it wasn't until people in that group grabbed me and said, "You're coming with us," and then they were the instigators of that relationship, that I really felt like I was part of that group. But I still find that it's hard for me to relax and go into social media because, I don't know, my brain is just business. I find that it's one of the things that I think I dislike the most about myself because I feel it holds me back. I can easily get up in front of a classroom full of kids. It's harder for me to, I think, create . . . I watch these theater teachers who are drama mamas, right? Everybody's like, "I'm your mom," and "Oh, I love you." And kids shower them with gifts and praise and things like that. And while I get, "You helped me get through high school" and "I'm really connected to what we do," I don't have that close of relationships with students. And I don't know if that's a boundary thing, as far as being male in a largely female-dominated subject area. But it's something that I'd like to do more about. It always feels like I'm keeping myself removed. But, I mean, I think I do good work. People say I do good work. So that's kind of what got me here, I think.

What is one of your most humorous moments being an introverted educator?

I don't know that I have one because it's not . . . I think a lot of people own their extrovert personality or they own their introverted personality. When I look online and I see comics or memes about introverted people, it's almost like a badge of honor that they wear. And it's something that I don't like, and it's really hard for me to find humor in it because it's wrapped up with anxiety and a little bit of depression. And I've dealt with imposter syndrome, which is a big one. It's really not something that I've been able to find humor in. It's painful, and I feel that it sets a lot of roadblocks in my way. One is living in this town where we have two high schools. One school that predominantly is athletics, or at least that's the public perception. If you want to throw a ball, you go to this high school. But if you want to go to college, you go to another high school.

And I see kids who are in the arts year after year choose to go across town. And I think that kind of feeds into that imposter syndrome because, at first it was, "Well, they've got a teacher there who's been doing it for 30 years." And for 30 years, if you wanted to do theater, you went over here because they were going through theater teachers at my school every four years, and none of them were really into what they were doing . . . So yeah, I wish I could find more humor in it, but it's painful.

How has being introverted yourself helped you to work with more introverted students?

I recognize them, I think, a lot better than a lot of teachers do. I think that a lot of teachers think that if you are not outspoken, if you are not participating and raising your hand, you're either not into it, you have a bad attitude, or you're not paying attention. And I don't jump to that automatically because I know . . . I mean, I'm in a subject area where you're graded on your ability to get up in front of a group of people and put yourself out there. And I know how hard that is. I know how emotionally paralyzing it can be. So, I like to focus a lot on exercises that get students out of their heads because I find that's pretty much the problem or the obstacle for those students. It's the, "Everybody's looking at me, everybody's laughing at me. What do I do if I mess up?" I mean, it's that fear of rejection and that fear of making mistakes.

So, one of the first things that I do in class gives them the freedom to fail. One of the phrases that I use with my kids a lot is, "You're going to fail often, and every time you do, we're going to celebrate it." So, if you make a big choice and you fall on your face, "Yeah. Good job. We love that." And so, when students mess up, we applaud. It's something that we celebrate because that's part of learning that I think a lot of us . . . And I think education is getting around to that now, about recognizing. But when I started, our motto at the middle school was that failure is not an option.

And I looked at the principal . . . or the assistant principal who told me that, who's now the superintendent . . . and I said, "What are you talking about? It absolutely is an option, and it's necessary." How else do you learn? And if you tell kids that failure is not an option, then when they do fail, what's the message that you're giving them? Before kids even get up in front of each other, we do a lot of prep work and breathing exercises. I use some yoga and some meditation, just some self-centering exercises to get the physical symptoms down.

We do a lot of play and a lot of games because I find that when kids are playing or when they're working towards an objective, it gets them outside of their heads more. The first thing that we do that's an acting exercise is pantomime so they don't have to talk. And it's an action that they have a lot of practice doing, so it's something they choose. And I try to put as much choice on the students as possible, within the parameters of the assignment, so that they have more ownership of what they're doing, rather than me prescribing it or putting it on them so that when I then have to do that as a director, there's more trust involved, and it's not like I'm just throwing them out there and saying, "Go for it."

I thought of a question, and I didn't want to share it until now, just because I wasn't sure if you'd come back to it. But you had mentioned earlier about how when you got into that more middle school age where kids started becoming meaner, and that's when a lot of those introverted tendencies . . . And you said you can usually spot introverted students.

Have you ever been able to intercept or help some of those situational, introverted behaviors just because you recognize them?

Yeah. I had a student in particular who . . . This was maybe three, or four, years into teaching theater. She came in, and I did not hear her say more than two words until we did the first vocal assignment, which was reading a poem. And when she did, it was . . . I mean, I don't even remember if she did that assignment. I think she might have refused, and she refused most of the public performance activities that first year. And when I saw her in the second year, I was like, "What are you doing? You hated this class. Why are you here?" And she came in the second year, which is usually a smaller group, and they're the kids who really want to be in there, and she kind of stepped out of her closet a little bit. It was just a little. And then each year I got to see her become more and more confident. By the time she was a senior, she was up in front of the class doing just amazing work.

And now I see her, she's . . . A lot of theater teachers will say, "Well, I have students who perform on Broadway," or "They're teachers," or "They do this." And she's one of my biggest success stories. She works at McDonald's. And I pulled up one morning to get some breakfast, and I heard this cheery voice, "Welcome to McDonald's. How are you today? What can I get you?" And I'm like, "That's a really happy person for 6:30 in the morning." I roll up, and there she is standing at the window.

She opens it up, "Mr. S, how are you?" I mean, just effusive and happy and just open. And I can tell this is the way she is with all of the customers that come through there. And this is 180 degrees away from where she was when she was in high school. And I was lucky, I had her younger sister this year. She came to one of the parent-teacher conferences, and I got to brag to her mother about how much this kid has grown and how proud I am of her.

The kids who come in have been doing it all, have been doing children's theater and blah, blah, blah. I love those kids – they're great. They make my job easy. But those kids who went from not being able to really talk to anybody at all, to being, I mean, just open and comfortable and happy, that is what I think is the best thing about my job. I would love to have kids who become professional actors, but really having people who are comfortable enough in their own skin to be able to talk to other people, which is something I have a challenge doing, that is what I think is the most successful thing I can do.

What are some ways that you've helped create that magic and brought your classroom to life?

The theater is magic. I mean, yeah, you can take a script. But even if you don't have a script, you get to create things with other people that didn't exist before. You get to share those things with an audience, and then once they're done, they're gone, they're ephemeral. And that magic, it's not a tangible piece of art that you can look at and appreciate. It's up here and it's in here. And it's those moments where I have students who work really hard on something and they're able to pull it off and become more successful than they ever thought they could be. That's where I find the magic. Magic is when we're playing a game and everybody's into it and just having fun with it. Or we work on improvisational theater, and they create really emotional moments of connection that aren't necessarily about jokes but are just about that joy of creation.

It's the best thing about my job because . . . I could've been that history teacher, but I think I make more connections with students . . . Empathy is one of my biggest things. And what I wanted as a history teacher is for kids not only to see how our system works but also to understand that we're part of a community, made up of a lot of different people. And that you need to understand that not everybody lives the same way you do or grew up the same way you do or feels the same way you do or worships the same way you do or votes the same way you do. And even if they don't, it's okay. You can understand where they're coming from because everybody wants to be healthy, everybody wants to be happy, and everybody wants to be loved.

And I don't know that you can do that. I don't know that you can really get that in a history class. I think some kids can. Talking about civil rights did that for me. But a lot of kids, it's just like, "Yeah, whatever. I want to take the test." But in a theater classroom, that's what the subject area is. It's creating empathy. You've got to empathize with a character that you're playing that is not in your experience.

And I think creating those moments of empathy, that's magic. I think that's what changes people. I think that's what our society needs more of. And I think that's what introverts are really good at because we internalize things. I mean, if somebody is upset with me, I think, as an introvert, I internalize that a lot. Extroverts are just like, "Yeah, whatever. You do you. I'm doing me. Yay!" But I sit there and agonize over it a bunch. I still agonize over things that happened 20 years ago. The key, I think, is getting extroverts to empathize and getting introverts to also empathize and then express that. That's magic.

Do you think a kindergarten teacher or a 5th-grade teacher could bring some of what you just spoke about into their classrooms?

Yes! The fact that, in teacher education, I mean, especially in elementary education, you've got to take the art section. You've got to include a little bit of the music thing. There is no class about theater in the elementary classroom. We have theater standards. I don't know if any of the elementary school teachers use them or if any principals say, "Oh, yeah. You have to meet these theater standards as well." But absolutely. And the benefit to that is so much more than putting on a play. It's that collaboration. It's working with different types of people and different opinions toward that shared goal. That collaboration, creative problem solving, public presentation, it's all of those jobs . . . I mean, you go through those 21st-century job skills that we're told that we need to give students, and theater does it, I think, better than just about any other subject area, but we don't look at it that way.

Our education system looks at it as, "Well, that's fun, and playing dress up and playing pretend is fun, but it's not a real school." I think if elementary educators had to take a class in theater in the classroom, it would help them in so many ways. I mean, just using theatrical play and activities to activate other lessons gives . . . because you don't remember the content in school, you remember the experiences. I mean, I remember the first day of school, my teacher Ben Gillis, junior year of American history, playing "We Didn't Start the Fire" and having us write our own version with historical events from our lifetime. I remember it 30 years later.

I remember the school plays and I remember the concerts, but I don't remember sitting in class learning about Manifest Destiny. I mean, I had it in my memory, but it's not something I actively go, "Oh, yeah. I remember when I did that." And I think that if we had more of those experiences in school, I think number one, you'd get kids a lot more activated, especially those kinesthetic learners. And I think the more you get outside of the school model, it just helps in so many ways. And I think it's not something that's even on our radar.

Reflection questions to ponder

What did you find most relatable or inspiring about Zach's story?

How might you apply the takeaway about working with introverted students?

2

Meet Sara

An introverted elementary educator with a heart to celebrate everyone

I have lived in Wyoming for 21 years. This is my seventh year in the elementary classroom and my eleventh year in education. Being confident is not something I get accused of often, but I think that is one of the funny things about being an introvert. I can feel completely confident and comfortable, but confidence is not something that I show others.

When I was in high school, I was part of a group putting on a camp for other teenagers. There was a lot of talk about leadership. One person said they wanted me to give the talk about it. Everyone kind of chuckled. I seemed like an odd choice for a leader. But I agreed all the same. I put together a speech on quiet leadership: quiet leadership, quiet service, quiet power. This is something that has carried with me into the classroom, creating that "quiet" magic for my students.

Tell me about your journey that brought you to education. How did being more introverted impact this journey?

I always loved kids. When I was probably 5 or 6, I had two little girls that were younger than me that I enjoyed helping take care

DOI: 10.4324/9781003321750-3

of. I did the "play school" thing with my toys, where I was the teacher and my toys were the students. I remember looking up to teachers or older kids who helped take care of younger kids. I thought they were so interesting. I wanted to be fun and exciting like they were. And that, I think, is the first time I wondered if I could be a teacher. When I was in middle school, I started helping with church activities and leading things for younger kids. The thing is, there was always this underlying stress. I didn't want to be noticed or seen. I didn't mind doing things when it was just the kids, but if anyone else was around, that changed everything for me.

When I was at the end of 8th grade, I made the decision to become a teacher. My parents tried to talk me out of it. They said I would never be able to buy that Ford Mustang I wanted. They made some jokes about the life of a teacher. It was kind of ironic. I didn't like school. It was hard for me. I had to work twice as hard as my brother to get mediocre grades. Along the way, I had a few teachers, though, who never made it feel like there was something wrong with me. They let me know that it was okay. Sometimes people just learn differently.

A piece of being an introvert for me is needing time to think and process. So often during a school day, we are rushed. We don't have time for thinking and processing. I like to be very sure of what I say before I say it. And so, when I look back at growing up, three things really stand out that have formed me as a teacher.

The first is to be the kind of teacher that can say to a kid, "What if I said it to you a different way?" Math was my hardest subject. There was a teacher in my high school who everyone warned me not to take. They said he was mean and gave a lot of homework. A mean math teacher who gave a lot of homework just didn't sound like a good recipe to me. I avoided his class for the first three years of high school. Then I found myself in his class. I found he wasn't mean or scary – at least not if you worked hard, which is always something math teachers told my parents. "I just don't understand. She works so hard; she just isn't getting it." Well, this "scary" math teacher got it. He could tell when he said something that I didn't get. He would say, "I lost you, didn't I?" and I would nod. Or he would say, "What if we tried this?" or "What if I said it this way?" I would have to take my younger brother to school for his zero-hour Trig class, and often this teacher would see me sitting in the commons and ask if I wanted practice. So, I would go to his classroom, and he would have Styx playing, and I would work on algebra while he graded or did whatever else he needed to. This teacher really saw me.

This is the next thing I have tried to bring into my classroom – a willingness to see past behavior or academic struggle, to see the person and what they need. Feeling dumb or like you aren't good enough is awful. So, I try to always make sure I find and celebrate the good in every student I encounter. I also try to meet them where they are, not where they should be.

Finally, the third thing that is so important to me is to give kids time to think and grow. I absolutely maintain high expectations. And, giving students an environment that celebrates thinking, not just achievement and correct answers, is something that I hope helps all my students to grow. These are the types of classrooms that I thrived in most. They are the ones that inspire me and the classroom that I hope to have for all the students who walk through my door.

What are some ideas you have for other teachers to celebrate thinking? Would celebration for 5th grade be different from kindergarten?

I always let students choose celebrations. They can create one or ask for one that we have already created. I think this part can look the same in all grades. I had a student a few years ago ask for a "mermaid cheer." So, we worked together to figure something out. I still have kids request that one. It was a 2nd grader who came up with it, and to this day, even 5th graders love it. Silly and cheesy are great celebrations for all ages.

What is one of your most humorous moments being an introverted educator?

I don't know that I can necessarily say this is a funny moment. But being an introvert in a very loud world, you develop other means of communication. I can remember sitting in a meeting that was rapidly deteriorating into chaos. One of my other quiet friends and I locked eyes. We didn't say a word. I don't even know that our expressions changed. After looking at each other for a few minutes, listening to the sheer volume around us, we both just started laughing. We understood exactly what we were thinking. And it just struck us as very funny that such a big deal was being made about something that should not have ended the world. Rather than try to speak, we had a silent conversation, and it was nice to share that with someone who understood.

What is one of your most challenging moments being an introverted educator?

One of my most challenging times as a teacher is meetings. The pressure to speak and be ready for anything is incredibly hard. I like time to think. I want to understand a topic fully before having to speak on it. The worst part is, though, when I finally do have the courage to speak and the response I get is, "What did you say, Sara?" There were a few years where it seemed like every meeting I attended, people talked over each other and over the presenter. I cannot tell you how many times I worked up the courage to speak and was asked to repeat myself, only to have others continue their conversations over the top of what I was saying. It made me feel very small. Insignificant. As if anything I could possibly have to share wasn't worth noticing. I felt this constant battle between "Have courage, speak up. Be a part of this conversation" and "It doesn't matter. No one wants to hear your ideas."

Being introverted, I often feel awkward and out of step with people. Being a teacher, I think I feel this pressure to be outgoing and charismatic. That just isn't me though. I am most comfortable in my classroom with my students, learning and growing and being curious. So many times, with other teachers and sometimes parents, the pressure to be something I am not can be a very heavy feeling.

How has being introverted yourself helped you to work with more introverted students?

I think being introverted has helped me because I understand the kids who are often overlooked or considered odd. It's easy to celebrate and get along with the kids who always want to answer questions and be noticed. It's not always easy to connect with the quieter kids.

I have lunch with my students often. One time I was eating lunch with three kids. Two kids were getting their lunch, so it was just me and one student. This was one of my quiet kids. We sat there for seven minutes in complete silence, and that was okay. So often quiet kids are forced to talk or be more outgoing than they want to be. That seven minutes of silence was perfectly fine. We were comfortable and when the other kids joined, the silence ended, but that's okay, too.

Are there ways that you've been able to create magic in your classroom and bring your classroom to life?

One of the best compliments I have ever received was when a student's mom thanked me for "truly seeing her child." She said that she appreciated that I really knew her child and that I saw them for who they are. That meant the world to me. And it got me wondering if maybe that was my gift – to see the real child.

With that in mind, I have always tried to make my classroom an environment where all students felt comfortable. Where taking a risk or sharing an idea is something to be valued and celebrated.

I think that is my brand of magic. To see kids as they are and help them have the courage to take a risk with their own ideas.

What are some of the strategies or ways you have made all students feel comfortable in your classroom?

I don't know that it is so much an activity as it is a process. First and foremost, we celebrate each other in my class. Being introverted, I understand how kids feel about talking in front of classmates. I make it a policy that everyone talks in my class. I scaffold this with lots of turn-and-talk opportunities. But then I do require all kids to speak when called on. From that mindset, I encourage kids to clap or celebrate each other for taking risks. Being an introvert and always being allowed to rely on teachers not expecting you to talk or having classmates talk for you is not helpful in the long run. This is with the goal of helping all students to be confident speakers.

Writing notes is something I have started doing that really seems to help students feel good in my classroom. I have seen notes stay in pencil bags for months, and parents have told me about kids asking for a note to be hung above their bed or on the refrigerator. It's simple, but it lets all kids know that I see them.

Reflection questions to ponder

What did you find most relatable or inspiring about Sara's story?

How might you apply the takeaway about working with introverted students?

3

Meet Aaron
An introverted educator who finds power in discussion

For me, talking about myself may be the epitome of an introvert. I find it difficult, but I love to talk about big ideas or issues (which is probably strange considering sharing an idea or opinion today leaves me more vulnerable to criticism than simply stating a few words about my background). This brings me to the overall point of this introduction – I am a recovering history teacher who has spent 12 years in a classroom. I say recovering due to the fact I have now transitioned to the role of a school counselor and have spent two years in this new role. Sometimes I wake up in the middle of the night hearing the call of the classroom and feeling the pull to return.

Tell me about your journey that's brought you to education. How did being more introverted impact this journey?

So, I think my journey is a little more nontraditional than typical. I'm a first-generation college student. I went to college, but that was not my plan initially, anyway. I grew up in a household where the idea was to just work, get a job, that kind of thing. But I was fortunate enough to get a wrestling scholarship

DOI: 10.4324/9781003321750-4

and went to a community college, and that was my first taste of college, but I was a terrible student. . . . That transition from high school to college was kind of rough for me at first, especially first-generation college. I didn't realize how tough that was on me, initially, compared to the other people who it's just the plan. That's what you did.

In high school, I had to sign up for the Wyoming Army National Guard Program, and my plan was that I would do that because I could still drill one weekend. I went to basic training between my junior and senior year of high school, and then after I graduated, I could just go active duty. That was my original plan, and then I got this wrestling scholarship that completely changed my trajectory. Now, this was just before 9/11. So, I lived one year at the community college, came back the following year, and then the September 11 attacks happened. Then being in the National Guard was no longer that part-time, one-weekend-a-month type of deal.

I did one major deployment to the Middle East to Iraq in 2004, but in between 9/11 and that, there's several things that we did for security for the Olympics and Salt Lake City in 2002, and things like that. And all that kind of broke up my college experience so it took me, basically, eight years to get a bachelor's degree because of it all.

So, it kind of gave me some perspective, but in terms of getting into education, it was not something that . . . I mean, it didn't come to me as a 3rd grader that I wanted to be a teacher. I always enjoyed history, and it was like, "How can I take some-thing that I enjoy, still work with that in some way?" So that's how I ended up majoring in social studies education so that I could teach history. In terms of being an introvert, I don't know that initial journey . . . I don't know that it either helped or hindered it necessarily. Once I got that clarity and focus, I think it probably helped me because then I was able to channel that being alone and accomplishing things. It was easy for me to ignore people, I guess.

Once it was like, "Yeah, this is definitely what I'm going to do. I'll do whatever it takes to finish," then it was like easy to shut off outside distractions and just focus on what I need to do to accomplish my goals and make it through school. I think just overall, really, my experience in the military is what kind of drove me to and shaped who I am today. But it really prepared me to be a better student, and I think that experience helped me once I transitioned into the civilian world, teaching and working with students, being able to set goals and accomplish a mission, so to speak, and kind of translating that into, "I can help students with that as well."

What is one of your most challenging moments being an introverted educator?

In the classroom itself, it's incredibly draining as an introvert, and just the nature of the job itself, that can be a challenge where depending on the day – like if a lot is going on by your last block of the day – teaching that kid can be just exhausting. Then there are other days, and I haven't pinpointed what the difference is or what causes that to happen, but there's something that just happens and I feel energized. I feel great, and I haven't figured out what that is to bottle it up and figure out what I did. But I think, just in general, the job can be challenging because you are on stage interacting with people all day, answering 9,000 questions a day combined with having to present an engaging lesson.

But then you also have the perception of what society thinks a teacher should be, and that kind of is becoming ingrained in what administration and all these outside consulting companies think education should be. So, you have most movies that present a competent educator – it's somebody who's, like, doing some dramatic lesson or is funny or you know, and some of these outside companies and consulting firms have kind of taken that as well, "This is what we need to turn all teachers into." So, you get these different pieces of training, and you could pick one, but it doesn't matter what it is. But they want you to do these wild dramatic things to engage students.

Sitting through these training sessions, they're doing these things that made me feel physically uncomfortable to be in the room to have to participate in the process and then to go back to the classroom and that's the expectation that you're supposed to do. That's just not me. Personality-wise that doesn't fit with me and who I am, and it makes me feel deep down like, "Well, this is what I'm supposed to be. I'm just a failure as a teacher." This is kind of like the message that you get, but it's not the flare and the dramatics and everything else that causes somebody to be a competent, good teacher and get engagement. It's kind of missing the boat. Really, it's being able to develop a solid foundation and relationships with a student and a group of students.

It's the difference, not what you do at the moment. It's creating at the beginning of the year solid foundations, structure, classroom management, and all that, but then having positive relationships with as many students as possible and collectively having a positive classroom environment. Then, if you have that, it doesn't matter what the activity is. You can get students to do it, and it could be the most boring thing in the world, not that that was my goal, but it could be that, and students would do it because they trust you and respect you when you have that relationship.

Then it opens the door. Then you have conversations that are like, "Yeah, I really don't like this assignment. I did it, but can we do something different next time?" Just creating that trust that, "Yeah, we can have a conversation." Then through those conversations, as a teacher, I was able to develop things that they wanted to do and were excited to do and then that just further builds more trust, and you have a solid classroom.

Was there ever something you were able to do to make it your own just to meet that expectation?

A lot of expectations, to me, was checking boxes. It was never anything like, "I'm going to go back and I'm going to do this all the time." So it was, "What can I do when an administrator comes into the room and they're looking to check that box, what can I do at that moment that they check the box, and they leave me alone?"

It wasn't like I was looking to adopt anything that I could take in and create my own. I thought that it wasn't going to make me a better teacher because it all kind of seemed like window dressing anyway. That's not the thing that matters. It's having those good solid relationships. I know there was one thing where you have a class chant, clap on the table, or something like that.

I just kind of pared that down to the minimum where I would just have a clap that they would repeat to get their attention, and everybody would quiet down and focus on you and having those things I think is a good teaching practice. But I think that was enough in the ballpark that I could do with that. It was like, "Okay, yeah. They're doing something that they learned." Then you get left alone as a teacher, and it was really a shame. It's like that's what they focus on. . . . I always had really good evaluations and classroom management and everything else, and it wasn't anything that I took away from those extroverted things that made that happen. It was building relationships with students.

How has being introverted yourself helped you work with more introverted students?

I think it just kind of brings greater awareness of what it's like to be in their shoes. It creates empathy for those students. If you are doing an activity that requires the student themselves to be on stage, so to speak, or give a presentation, then it's easier for me to facilitate a conversation with them. I can say, "I understand. It's not easy for me either. What can we do to make it easier for you?" We still have the expectation that this is what's going to happen, but what can we do to adapt it that makes you more comfortable in that situation and somewhere as expectations get thrown at us? Adapting is something that can make it work for you . . . being able to facilitate conversations with students in the same way so that they could be more comfortable and more willing to participate more actively.

But then also having that understanding that not everybody in the classroom is going to be wanting to raise their hand

and ask questions and participate in the discussion, and that's okay sometimes. Just having the awareness that it's not always productive to force that student to engage. That doesn't mean they're not learning or that they're not getting it. It's just that's not how they learn and that's not always going to be productive to force the issue on them.

You mentioned that going through the military journey helped you to become more focused as an introvert. Could you explain that a little bit more?

I think introverts tend to recharge by being alone. Using that to achieve a goal is like, "Okay, I can just tell people that I need to get this done and I'm going to be alone, then use that to do what I need to do to finish school and homework papers or whatever."

Are there ways that you've been able to create magic in your classroom and bring your classroom to life?

I think there are two separate answers. One of them was when I personally felt like things were alive and the other was when students would think they were, so I think those are two different answers. Based on conversations with students, I know what they like and when they thought things were going good versus when we were doing things that I like and I thought they were going well. Anytime that I could choose a topic that I knew would engage students and I could connect it to something in their life in the United States and we could discuss that is when I felt like that was where the magic was happening. That was where the real learning was happening. Sometimes you can kind of create this magic with these small pockets in the classroom, but sometimes for some reason, this topic, the connection, whatever it was, we got to a point where everybody was engaged and everybody had a comment and question. To me, when those things happened and we were having a real discussion and conversation about what was happening, those were more magical moments. I think more learning was happening in those moments than anything else.

Now, students, on the other hand, may not see it that way. Some of them would enjoy those moments, but not everybody. History and social studies tend to be a subject, especially in middle school, that either you like it and you have an appreciation of it or you don't. It's really hard to get it with everybody else who doesn't. . . . So, one of the ways that I could do that is through simulations or a game-type activity. I've done one where they were broken up into teams and they had to simulate going on the Oregon Trail. They had to choose items to take with them, and then as they were going along, I had cards that were like, "Oh, you chose to go this way. But then you got lost for five days or whatever."

So based on their choices, they determined whether they were successful or not. Students really enjoyed doing things like that. They're still relevant. They're on topic. They're learning things, and that kind of creates that engagement for everybody else who doesn't have the same appreciation of the history. I think it's one of those subject areas that, as people age, they grow to appreciate more. It's just in middle school, especially, since it's not 50/50. People who like it or not, it's a lot smaller than that, but the people who are into it love it. Creating opportunities that can create some fun and excitement – that's what gets everybody so on board.

Reflection questions to ponder

What did you find most relatable or inspiring about Aaron's story?

How might you apply the takeaway about working with introverted students?

4

Meet Kate
An introverted educator who finds the most value in the small moments

I learned so much about myself from the 15 years I spent in the classroom, and I learned most of those things from my experiences and interactions with the thousands of students I had the good fortune to have pass through my life. While my first reaction is often to avoid human interaction, I have been inspired and encouraged to the good and potential in others and myself. This profession has proven rewarding for my career development and fulfillment, and I am proud of the work I have done and hope you will be, too.

Tell me about your journey that brought you to education. How did being more introverted impact this journey?

After I graduated from high school, I moved to Fort Collins, and I lived there for a year and just worked. Then I realized, "This is awful. I need to figure out something that I can do for the rest of my life that I will enjoy and will provide me some financial security," all those kinds of things. And I think that I chose teaching initially because it's something that I knew and was comfortable with.

DOI: 10.4324/9781003321750-5

That's probably a word that I use often is being comfortable. So as an introvert . . . I mean, I think most people seek comfort, but I often will run away from things that are uncomfortable – seeking comfort.

So, teaching seemed like the comfort of going through school. As a kid, I think that was one of the reasons we played school all the time and something that I said was, "Yeah, being a teacher, I would want to be a teacher." So that stuck with me.

When I chose English language arts, I think maybe it speaks more to my personality as an introvert and that . . . this isn't always true, but reading and writing – and especially reading for me – was always an escape, and it still is today.

When I am feeling overwhelmed, and that is a lot of the time, I can go and read a chapter in a book and then jump back into my life and kind of feel at peace again. That started for me at a very young age, and I think when I learned to read, I would sit down next to the bookcase and just go through these picture books.

I loved Shel Silverstein's books. I would just read those out loud to myself. That was my happy place. We'd be at my grandparents' house or something, and I would go hide behind my grandparents' chairs or kind of beside them, where I would be out of the way and just read these books. My love of reading really was immediate, and that was always my place of peace and calm.

In my undergrad, the first English class that you took was a literature class. We just did a lot of creative projects where there wasn't one right answer and you could do so many different things and still get it right. At that time, not having a lot of confidence, that gave me some confidence. It was okay that my answer didn't have to be this perfect answer, like the final answer in a math problem.

Some of the things I wrote for the literature class felt safe. It was calm, and it was freeing. Reading and writing, a lot of times, are done in isolation, but there was a lot of connection when I think back to my reading and writing experiences. Those were more intimate connections one-on-one, a lot of times. A couple that I remember . . . I mean, I remember reading books with my grandpa and just having that connection with him.

What I love about reading and writing is that there's no pressure. We can read a book together, and I don't have to come up with things to talk about. Or in class, I remember in my undergrad, in a writing class, sitting next to people and you had this task to work on, but you could also connect with people on a personal level. You could have these side conversations. You could have a conversation about the paper you were working on. It was kind of like a distraction, I guess. Reading and writing were always a little bit of a distraction and a way to connect with people, too, that didn't seem like, "I'm just trying to connect with this person," or "They are going to judge me on whether I get this problem right," or something like that. It has been both, I guess, isolating but then providing that connectivity, too.

What is one of your most humorous moments being an introverted educator?

It was a sophomore honors English class I was teaching, and I had this big class. They were all very driven students, and many of them were very extroverted.

They were writing stories, and I can't remember exactly, but they were writing stories together. This group had done this story, and they were sharing it. It was about a couple on a plane, and it kind of went almost . . . I took it in my mind as inappropriate, and then . . . it went to something about playing Jenga. They were playing Jenga together, but it was . . . I don't know. They went to the bathroom together or something like that.

I think it was always hard for me to . . . I guess in the classroom, when in front of the whole class, you have to kind of keep it together . . . I always felt like I had to. For a long time, I would say I wasn't willing to be vulnerable. In this moment, I was just cracking up. I was so embarrassed. It was kind of that moment we were all laughing. They were laughing so hard on the ground, and it was this moment that I could be vulnerable.

I think that at that moment, I was thinking, "We've got to get this stuff done, meet these standards," and it was getting back to that having fun and enjoying writing and reading and sharing and trusting them, and them trusting me and being vulnerable. In that moment, it got me back to that. I went up and down with being vulnerable and enjoying those moments. That was that outside pressure, which I felt a lot and felt like that I had to fit in a mold that wasn't really my personality. In moments like that, it got me back to being myself: "This is okay to have fun and to enjoy the writing and to laugh and cry."

Because some of those other moments, I think, and maybe not humorous, were when students were vulnerable in their writing and having those moments of vulnerability.

Some of my best moments as a teacher were working with students one-on-one or in small groups where we were talking about pieces of writing or pieces of literature and their own lives and lived experiences. And when they trusted me enough to write some deep stuff and they got some of those things on paper. Because some of the kids that I often thought had the most difficulty with writing had been through a lot and had maybe kept a lot of those things in. So, when they even started to get some of those things on paper, I mean, those were special moments.

Yeah, they were doing this story. I still see these kids today from this class, and we were reading a . . . I believe it was a play, and it was using a metaphor for the woman's eyes, like that they were as bright as the streetlights or something like that, but it never really says her eyes. I said that it was her eyes, and they argued with me that it was her breasts. I was like, "What?" And I just said, "Your guys' minds are in the gutter." But they're 10th graders. But they still argue with me about that today, and I think they're like 27 now.

What is one of your most challenging moments being an introverted educator?

I think the challenge . . . I mean, there are a lot of challenging moments for introverts. It's exhausting . . . for a long time, it was that I was trying to be somebody else. . . . I think it's changed a lot today . . . But being an introvert is okay. This is who I am. I like who I am. And these are the things I need to do for myself, especially after a long day.

But the challenge . . . I mean, I worked in a small district for my whole teaching career, so for 14 years. And then a lot of that comes with a lot of extra duties outside of the school day. Just being around people and putting myself out there all day long, just in an eight-hour day, that's really exhausting for me. And then I need that recharge time and to come home and just have quiet time, but a lot of the times that wasn't the case. It was a 14-year challenge for me to come to terms with, I guess, realizing who I was and taking care of myself and not thinking that I must meet other people's demands of things that weren't healthy and balanced for me. Every day putting so much of yourself out there that I need time every day to recharge.

I've done those personality tests many times. My husband and I, before we got married, we did the religious counseling, and they go through the whole Myers-Briggs and do the personality testing, the big 200 question one or whatever. I remember husband telling me the introverted one, "You're almost in the danger zone. You're almost clinical." I remember feeling bad about that – that there was something wrong with me. I think at that time, I was always trying to get out of my being an introvert, and I just fought against it so much. But it was such an important part for me to find that being an introvert is okay. I really like it and just accept it and figure out how to make my life work.

How has being introverted yourself helped you to work with more introverted students?

I want to say that I was patient and understanding, and I know that there were times when I wasn't. I mean, I've been trying to, a lot of that time, be an extrovert, and so trying to make other people extroverts, too. I think I spent some time thinking that that's what the goal was.

I loved those individual conferences, and that's what I did a lot because that worked for me, and I got great results for that.

And I think that those kinds of things helped those students who were introverts. An English language arts classroom, a lot of times, helps introverts because you're doing so much reading and writing. I think I did see myself as some of those students who weren't as outgoing, and that was okay because that was me.

Were there ways that you worked to make students more comfortable, knowing that that helped you?

I think that sometimes we would go write in different places or read in different places. Always offering options. Always offering a choice and the freedom to choose different ways of expression. And a lot of times, not just in writing, but in different kinds of creative projects or poetry. Not having to write or share. There was always a choice about sharing. They never had to share with a class or with a partner or peer editing. That was one thing for me as a student that I wasn't very comfortable with, so I often let them choose partners instead of picking partners for them, and sometimes it was somebody outside of the class. I think I tried to do those things to fit different personalities.

Did you ever create moments in your classroom that offered chances for those students to recharge?

I don't know if I . . . I did not ever intentionally say, "This is a time for . . . We're going to set aside 10 minutes, and this is a moment where we all get to decompress and kind of realign ourselves." I included those things like writing time, just free writing time. Or there always was the choice to draw or to do that in different ways, that expression. Yeah, just kind of free reading time. Those are the things that come to my mind.

Are there ways that you've been able to create magic in your classroom and bring your classroom to life?

I guess I tried to incorporate as much choice as possible. Going back to the beginning when I talked about freedom and creativity and being able to choose how you present something, how you demonstrate something. But doing projects that they got to choose how to do and bringing things to life through different art mediums. I've had kids do just some amazing, amazing things through poetry, through those shadow boxes (I see those a lot these days). Through notebooks and just combining all kinds of different ways of expression instead of maybe just the ways that require just speaking.

I know I was supposed to be meeting the standards and doing all this writing, and maybe sometimes I was more interested in a love of reading or an appreciation of reading and writing than meeting the standards and in giving those other opportunities as much attention as I could.

Reflection questions to ponder

What did you find most relatable or inspiring about Kate's story?

How might you apply the takeaway about working with introverted students?

5

Meet Jasmin
An introverted elementary ESL teacher building a safe and supportive environment

I am a teacher who loves small group structures, engaging projects, meaningful learning, personal touches, and a calming atmosphere. Every chance I get to make a connection with a student is a chance worth taking, even with the growing pressures and time constraints teachers now face. Just like there is no one way for kids to learn, there is no one way for teachers to teach. I hope that by sharing my story as a part of this book, it will help other introverted teachers feel comfortable being themselves, knowing that what they have to offer is valuable even if it doesn't include dancing on tables and shouting it from the rooftops.

Tell me about your journey that brought you to education. How did being more introverted impact this journey?

As a child I was always terrified of any situation in school that required me to "stand out" from others in the class. When I think back to pretty much all my school years, the first word that probably comes to mind is stress. I was always stressed out! I worried about getting called on, about having to do activities that put me

DOI: 10.4324/9781003321750-6

at the center of attention, and about doing poorly and everyone seeing or knowing.

When I was in 3rd grade, I had a teacher that I thought was the most amazing woman ever to walk the Earth. She was quiet and kind and soft spoken. She played acoustic guitar, and she made me a seat pocket out of an old pair of jeans that I still have to this day and use in my own classroom. I felt like she loved me, even though I was so painfully shy, and I wanted nothing more than to please her, so I began to come out of my shell. I remember loving that year of school. Fast forward to junior high.

My family moved, and I was new to a town, new to a school, and taking a big step from elementary school to junior high. This can be enough to put a painfully shy, introverted student right over the edge, but much to my surprise, I survived it all and found my place. My science teacher that year was an older man who didn't waste words, smiled a lot, and gave quiet compliments. He made each student feel special, smart, and adored. He had a way of making learning fun by making it *so* challenging. He was an incredible teacher who made me enjoy science for the first time in my life. He also showed me that I had a lot to offer by just being me. I can't say that my stress over school ever went away over the years, but I can say that I started to understand that it was okay that I didn't love the activities that other kids seemed to love. I figured out what situations worked for me and what situations didn't work so well for me, and I use those ideas to steer me in life and appreciate other people like myself.

After college, I started out in the greenhouse industry with a degree in horticulture and business management. I imagined spending my days growing plants in a nice peaceful greenhouse that I owned and operated.

I had a car accident, though, and it became clear that I needed to rethink my options. I began working as an educational support personnel for high school age students with special needs. My mom and soon-to-be husband were both teachers, and they encouraged me to go back to school and do the same. Being introverted, the thought of a chaotic classroom and being the leader of a whole group of kids did not sound like a fit for me, but unsure of what else to do, I moved forward with it. Turns out, there are plenty of ways to create a classroom that fits my introverted personality. Teaching is one of those professions where you really are in charge of your own space, and as long as you are getting done what you are intended to get done, you can do it in an atmosphere and a manner that fits your own teaching style. As soon as I figured this out, I began planning the ways in which I would create a classroom that made me feel comfortable.

So, you are probably wondering why an introvert would decide to become a teacher? It is a profession where you literally put yourself on stage in front of a group and lead the learning. Well for me, I didn't jump into it with open arms; instead, it kind of came to me. All of you introverts reading this are like, "Ahhh, that sounds wonderful," right? I started to understand that not all teachers were extroverts. There were others like me and plenty of students like me, too. We needed each other! Throughout my entire life, I tried to fit in a mold meant for someone else. I tried. Then I met LeeAnn. She was a teacher whose classroom was quiet, calm, cozy, happy, and positive. She taught children in such a calm and kind manner that instantly felt like home to me. That was the kind of teacher I wanted to be.

When I saw the magic that she created without costumes, flashing lights, or jumping on tables I was sure I could do this. I felt comfort knowing that there was someone else out there like me, and that it was okay, and even great! Since then, I have worked to provide that experience for my students, too. A place where they feel safe, loved, appreciated, accepted, and, most importantly, comfortable. We laugh a lot, we bond, they know I love them, and we all learn all the time. I hope that by stepping out of my comfort zone and sharing with you some of my experiences being an introvert you can feel that same comfort and acceptance that I felt or understand introverts a little bit better and figure out how to access their strengths.

I began work as a 2nd grade teacher in a Title One school then moved to kindergarten. Our school loops (moves with kids from one grade to the next, so we have them for two years), so then I taught 1st grade as well. I taught K–1 for several years until I became a mom.

At that time, I was looking for something a little more flexible and part-time, so I became an interventionist in the same school, working with small groups of struggling students in reading and math.

Now I am working as an ESL teacher, helping students who speak English as a second language find success in their learning by alleviating the language barrier. I am loving the combination of having my own group of students just like I did as a classroom teacher, but I work with them in small groups throughout the day. I can connect with them and their families at a very personal level, just like I enjoy the most.

What is one of your most humorous moments being an introverted educator?

I can think of lots of moments, but not necessarily ones of humor, but one that I remember emotionally. Letting the class take the lead in discussions while I sat back and watched things unfold worked to my benefit. When kids hear something from me it might only partially sink in, but when they hear the same thing but from a friend, they are all in.

I can also think of students who were so painfully shy and introverted that when they were put on the spot, they would just panic. Just confiding in them that it is okay to feel that way and letting them know that I feel the same way in that situation, too, relieves a visible amount of tension. I never heard from anyone in my whole life that it was okay to be introverted, and even a strength, until I was well into adulthood. I wonder how it would have impacted me and changed my developing confidence to hear this from an adult when I was younger.

What is one of your most challenging moments being an introverted educator?

For me, the most challenging moments are those when I am asked to get up and "perform" in front of others. For example, our school does chants and cheers in smaller groups in front of the whole school at various times throughout the year.

Knowing how difficult these moments are, how have you helped to support your students in these difficult moments?

Connecting with kids and letting them know they aren't alone in their feelings is so valuable. Personally, when I am aware of a situation that is going to make me uncomfortable, I can prepare my thoughts, my reactions, and my mind for how I am going to get through it. I think it is important to do the same for our students. Give them warning, options, and encouragement in tough situations. A simple thing like a buddy can make all the difference in their comfort and willingness to participate.

I find these displays to be mortifying and stressful as opposed to motivating and inspiring as they are intended to be. I am sure that there are students out there who share my same trepidation and can feel motivated and inspired without getting up and dancing and yelling in front of 300 people.

How did you create an environment so students who were quiet would want to share?

Creating an environment where kids feel safe to share is key for quieter kids in the class. It is essential to model kindness, reward kindness and respect toward others, and redirect any negativity. I always tell students that we are a team or a family. Everything we do needs to support all our teammates because we are stronger and more successful together. I always have some type of community reward system going so students encourage others and genuinely want everyone to succeed. If we have this strong community in place, students know it is okay to be an active member in it because they trust that everyone will be kind and accepting in return.

How has being introverted yourself helped you to work with students who are more introverted?

Being a quieter person, I love to connect with kids personally. I think that going out of my way to make small, quiet connections with kids is invaluable. These don't have to be big gestures, just quick personal conversations, comments, or even a hug. Hearing your stories, insecurities, or personal comments makes kids feel that you are in it together. They will see you as a regular old person, too.

In that same regard, making sure to connect with kids personally when I need to redirect them, instead of calling them out in front of others, is also important. This isn't always possible, but I have found that, if possible, it is almost always far more effective because you maintain mutual respect and trust with a student.

Time spent building relationships with kids is never time wasted. In my experience, it pays back tenfold to take that 15 minutes at the beginning of the day to hear the stories about their dog, or their sister, or the dream they had last night, or how they are feeling about something, or whatever. Seeing that you care and giving kids a chance to share something important to them builds that student-teacher rapport, making students *want* to work for you, *want* to succeed for you, and *want* to meet your expectations. This is invaluable in the long run.

Probably most importantly, I know that just because someone isn't saying something, it doesn't mean they don't have something valuable to share. They might have the most insightful ideas in the group and just might need me to find the right way for them to share it. As a teacher, I work hard to create situations where students don't have to feel the stress that I once felt in school.

Reflection questions to ponder

What did you find most relatable or inspiring about Jasmin's story?

How might you apply the takeaway about working with introverted students?

6

Meet Jill

An introverted educator who finds richness in teaching business

Whenever I complete the "Am I an Introvert or Extrovert?" questionnaires, the results always reveal introvert. I force myself to portray self-confidence when being introduced or when asked to be a spokesman even though I'd rather others do that while I help generate the momentum to complete the task! I'm a business teacher with over 30 years of teaching experience who enjoys hiking in the mountains or strolling along the ocean beaches and spending time with my husband, adult children, and new grandson.

Tell me about your journey that brought you to education. How did being more introverted impact this journey?

Looking back at my childhood, I was the youngest of four, but the closest sibling to my age was almost a seven-year difference. So, growing up, I was always aware that I was very much an only child when I was playing, or even doing work, because everybody else was so much older than I was. I lived in rural Nebraska with parents who were farmers, so my parents were always around because they were either in the house having a meal or

DOI: 10.4324/9781003321750-7

working outside. It's not like there weren't people around, but it really was just my parents. And because we were farmers and we lived in the country, our nearest neighbors were probably close to four miles away. I really was very used to doing things by myself.

When I was a senior in high school, there were 26 kids in grades 9–12. I mean, we're talking so tiny. But everybody knew everybody. I knew . . . Well, you just knew everybody in the community. That's hard for people to understand unless they've experienced that. And you knew their relatives and you knew what church they went to, and all of that.

And so, since it was so tiny, if our school had an activity, that really meant that everybody did that activity. In 5th grade, I started playing a musical instrument. Then by the time I was in high school, I was in band and choir, and for a couple of years, I was a cheerleader. Even though I'm a short person, I played volleyball and I played basketball. And there was a small group of us, I think four of us, that did our senior yearbook. I mean really, whatever was offered, we took advantage of. And I don't remember ever taking a personality test or ever having a conversation in any class about being an extrovert or an introvert.

It took several years after high school for me to realize that maybe I was introverted. I don't know, I never really thought about it. I did know that when I went to college it was hard for me to join groups. People had told me, "You need to join groups." So, I joined a couple of student organizations, but probably, if people had a video or if they had social media back then, they would see this awkward teenager trying to be involved, I would think. Looking back, 30 some years, I think that's what I would see is this awkward kid that didn't really know how to fit in. And I continued to try to do the things that I had done in high school.

I wasn't loud and obnoxious, but I did things. . . . We talk about everybody goes to college now, but population, student population at that time was, maybe, pushing almost 14,000 at Kearney. Whereas today I think they have close to 7,000 students. But there had been this real big push for students to go to college. Or I don't know why we all went to college, but we did. So, one time I walked into a classroom – it was an English classroom

– and Dr. Smith was the teacher and it was an English literature course. And these were regular size classrooms, but at that
time, in the middle to late '80s, everybody went to college. But
I went to walk into this classroom of this great teacher and the
classroom was standing room only. So, there were maybe 25, 30
seats available. Of course, they were all full. And there were kids
everywhere, and not even in the classroom yet, just over full.
Kids sitting on the floor and whatever.

I didn't say anything and the teacher wasn't there yet. I just
looked around the room. I saw that there was a trash can close
to the teacher's desk, so I walked up to the front of the room,
took the liner out of the can with the trash in it, tied it shut so
I wouldn't spill, put that down on the floor, flipped it over, and
sat on it. All without saying a word, to not get noticed.

I guess even then I didn't realize that I was introverted or . . .
I don't know. Because I don't feel as though I got stepped on, but
I was nervous or afraid to say things.

A couple of years after I started college, I got married and
my husband started school. And I knew, when he started school,
I was like, "Okay, this is what you need to do. You've kind of
picked out a major so that means you're going to go to class.
You're not going to skip class. You're going to get to know your
professors, you're going to get involved with student activities,
you're going to make contacts, you're going to go to conferences,
you're going to be a leader." It was almost like a list. I knew those
were the things that could make a difference. I just didn't really
know how to feel comfortable and do those things.

It's probably taken more than half of my career to be comfortable with being an introvert. I don't know. Can you be an
outspoken introvert? Or how about an introvert that acts? I don't
know. But that's where I feel like I am. I have the answers, I just
don't know how to get out there, put myself out there.

I was a teacher in one district for over eight years, and no one
from central services knew who I was. When I had taught over
eight years, the director of curriculum and instruction came to
my room to . . . Because somebody had said, "Hey, Jill would be
a good candidate to go to this conference." When he came to my
classroom and introduced himself to me, he said, "Oh, and so

you must be a new teacher," and I answered, "Actually, I've been here for over eight years." People didn't know who I was.

So, behind the scenes, I do things, I get things done, I think I have great relationships with kids, but probably my childhood really set me up to be who I am. Somebody else who's done all the research is going to tell me that, yes, that's true, or no, that's false. But I just think that if I needed things done, I did them myself. I didn't really need the recognition. I didn't want somebody to step on me. But it's interesting how all of that comes back to who we are as adults and especially in education.

What is one of your most humorous moments being an introverted educator?

Pretty early on in my career and really without questioning first-day activities and understanding the repercussions that could resolve from those activities, I did that toilet paper activity where students tear toilet paper off as they enter the classroom. And then once class starts, students must share one thing about themselves for every sheet of toilet paper they had pulled off. One sweet innocent little freshman came to my room, and because I knew her and her family, I encouraged her. I convinced her to pull off several sheets. I don't know, 10, 20, goodness, maybe even more sheets than that. And I thought it was funny, but once I explained the activity, I saw her shrink down in her chair.

I thought, "Oh my gosh, what did I do?" I'm sure as a freshman it was agonizing for her to just stand, let alone say many different things about herself. I recognized it when she was talking about it and then how she struggled. And so, eventually, I started kind of helping supplement what she was saying. Oh gosh, I felt horrible. That really was the first and only time that I ever did that activity. I still feel guilty about that. I'm not sure if that's the most humorous moment that involved being an introverted educator, but I most definitely put myself in her shoes as that was happening. I learned a lot. Now, when I think about that first-day activity, I try to come up with something where the kids really aren't put in the spotlight, just because I know what it's like to have been there, done that, and felt so uncomfortable.

Instead of a game like the toilet paper game, what are some first week icebreaker type games that you have found to be more suitable for quieter students?

For the past few years, I've used the same activity. Students complete a sheet with about 20 questions about themselves, like favorite food, favorite color, place they've visited they'd like to return to, favorite book, etc. They get about 10 minutes to complete the sheet. Then I line students up into 2 straight lines, with students facing each other (one to one) . . . and we do "speed dating" where they get 30 seconds to talk about themselves and the person across from them listens. Once I call "time," they swap roles. Once they've both spoken, one line moves one person down the line, and we start again. With 30 students, this takes about 20 minutes, so it is a great way to get students out of their seats and gives them a chance to meet everyone in class.

What is one of your most challenging moments being an introverted educator?

The first day of school is always challenging for me. Even with students that I already know, I still don't feel comfortable with them. And especially a classroom of students that I don't know, which is typically how it is now with teaching a required class. In a large class, with anywhere between 27 to 30 kids in that classroom, I struggle with being comfortable. I struggle with being comfortable with that first day of school activity.

Lecturing to students is not my ideal activity, but I also don't like chaos in my room ever. Finding a happy medium activity is always difficult. I'm not the only one that teaches financial literacy. We have three or four teachers who teach it. We all try to teach somewhat the same content. Even on the first day of school activity, or the first day of the semester activity, we try to do the same thing. Somebody might come up with an idea, and then

I'm like, "Oh, this is totally out of my comfort zone." I think it's really because I'm an introvert. I don't feel comfortable with it, so I struggle with that.

In addition to that first day that I deal with every semester, we have assignments where our students must give class presentations. Now, I could get up in front of kids, and I do that every day, and I don't struggle when I'm lecturing or we're working on things, but wow, asking my kids to get up and do a class presentation – that's hard for me. Many times, I just have the kids turn in their assignments electronically, and then I grade that.

I have tried to push myself out of that comfort zone. Watching them struggle is a struggle for me. It's not like the kids don't do a good job. I'm always amazed after we've watched 20 to 30 presentations. "Wow, my kids really knocked that out of the ballpark." I don't know. I just feel uncomfortable with them doing that. I don't want them to feel like they have to feel uncomfortable because I know there are some kids that are like, "Oh my gosh, I'd rather do any-thing other than present to my classmates." That's hard.

Sometimes, I'll have a kid come to me and say, "Hey, I really don't want to present." I do allow the students who approach me to do that little presentation in front of me. Instead of standing in front of the classroom, they really can just sit next to me in two chairs and do their presentation that way because I know that they struggle and that makes me uncomfortable while they struggle with that, too.

You mentioned not wanting students to ever feel uncomfortable. What are some signs you notice or ways you can begin to tell students are uncomfortable in your classroom?

Most high school students (probably all people in general) are not comfortable standing in front of class and speaking, so I don't do that. Instead, I use small groups (2–3 people) and have them work around the room as a team to complete the learning activity. Most of the time, I allow them to select their own groups. More recently, and on a regular basis, I've found that students act disinterested or act perturbed more often than uncomfort-able. I teach juniors and seniors, so most of the time when they're "paired" with another student, they do so willingly.

How has being introverted yourself helped you to work with more introverted students?

I don't like it when students feel uncomfortable. It makes me feel uncomfortable, too. I just don't like that. I know we all need to learn how to deal with uncomfortable situations. Even after close to 30 years. I don't like feeling uncomfortable because my students are uncomfortable, even though I recognize that as a character flaw. After all those years, I still can't get through it, so I like to allow students to make a choice of the learning activity they want to complete. Some kids like to work within a pair or group always, and it's not necessarily about only doing half of the work or a third of the work, they just like to work with other people and need that action all of the time happening.

Allowing students to pick and choose, it's all about their learning. Not every activity has to be done independently or not every activity needs to be done as a group, so I let them work sometimes on the things that they want to work on, whether it's independently or let them pick and choose, "Do I want one partner or two or three?" I really discourage groups larger than three, just because then I do think they get off task easily.

But I also like students to get up and move around during class time. Our classes are 80 minutes long and so just sitting for 80 minutes, yeah, no. Your brain goes to sleep, so I do like to find a time during that 80-minute segment when they really do have to get up. It doesn't mean that they have to work with somebody else but get up out of their chair, try to do some things where they go to a wall or two to get their information or complete that activity. Even if it is independently, let's get up and move – let's get involved with some active learning. And so, I try to let them pick and choose and force them out of their chair but that doesn't mean that they have to really work with one other person or a group of people. If they want to do the activity independently, then sure, more power to you because you don't always like to get out there and mingle with people.

Creating various activities that require students to get out of their seats and work either independently or with a group forces them to reflect on the different choices they would or do make regarding financial literacy. The magic is allowing students to work in a way they're uncomfortable with, which helps them complete that assignment. I believe that the students who see that they're in charge of their own learning begin to recognize empowerment, and maybe empowerment is magic, but it's not "magic." It's not a secret potion that I'm sharing with the kids or that I have.

So, the subject matter of financial literacy, truly, truly is 20% knowledge and 80% behavior. Now, I can't grade them on that 80% behavior. That's what happens outside of the classroom. But kids learn or students learn if they want to become better consumers. They now have that knowledge, and it's their own individual behavior that dictates their financial success. I just so truly believe that.

I can teach them how to create a budget. It's simple. You can use a budgeting app, or you can do a spreadsheet, or you can write it down on paper. That's what I teach in the classroom when we're budgeting. But if you want magic, if they want to make a change in their life, they have to apply it outside their classroom. And it's that magic that happens when they decide to implement their knowledge. They truly can see a direct correlation between creating a budget, sticking to it, and then ending up with the beginnings of that emergency fund that we talked about or a saving fund that allows them to spend money that they've already saved.

I try to convince them that they don't have to wait until they have that first full-time job to do that. If they have income, they can start to plan. Budget is not a four-letter word. Like, hello, let's make a difference in our life. And it's not that kids come with zero knowledge. That's part of it. We don't have to think about breathing to be a survivor in this world. It just happens.

It's the same thing with our money. You don't have to have all that knowledge. You don't have to think about your money and where it comes from and how to spend it. It just happens. But if you have the knowledge and you can streamline your behavior to have set goals, and you want to reach those goals, you can move mountains and that's the magic. And trying to convince the kids that each one of them has that magic within them. That's magic, but it's not "magic." It's just behavior.

Reflection questions to ponder

What did you find most relatable or inspiring about Jill's story?

How might you apply the takeaway about working with introverted students?

7

Redefining the meaning of class participation

I think that a lot of teachers think that if you are not outspoken, if you are not participating and raising your hand, that you're either not into it, you have a bad attitude, or you're not paying attention.

(Zach)

How can we redefine participation? Introverts participate in different ways than students who are more extroverted. For example, they might use reflection, which is answering a thoughtful question through a nonverbal response. However, educators often view participation as thinking out loud. Extroverts find this to be much easier, whereas introverts may struggle more or fail to participate in entirety (Higgin, 2017).

Participation is often conflated with thinking out loud, and that's something at which extroverts excel but introverts struggle. Participation can and should mean so much more: asking a thoughtful question, helping others, volunteering, coming to office hours or staying after class, posting in an online forum, doing revisions of work, and beyond.

"It is not always the biggest talkers that have the biggest ideas" (Cain, 2013a). Silence is not a problem. Embracing silence in teaching and participation can be done through an internal dialogue (Reda, 2009). This is the space students have between when the teacher asks a question or poses a prompt and the student speaking. This is a safe space for introverts to have time to

DOI: 10.4324/9781003321750-8

reflect. Participation is a direct reflection of how safe the students feel, Reda explains.

Participation could be more than the student raising their hand. Higgin (2017) suggests an online forum or something as simple as a Google Doc. Students can be given a question and respond to that question through the document instead of out loud, giving a student an opportunity, or even a choice, to think reflectively.

By utilizing technology and choice to allow students to participate, students do not need to share out loud. Other examples include setting up a recorded presentation instead of a live presentation or using a Google Classroom to contribute thoughts instead of sharing in front of everyone.

How might student silences be reframed as productive and useful? Strauss (2021) explains that educators must change their mindsets and allow students the opportunity to participate through other avenues, such as students "speaking" through a recorded text and multimedia presentation.

> Being a quieter person, I love to connect with kids personally. I think that going out of my way to make small, quiet connections with kids is invaluable.
>
> (Jasmin)

Building a rapport and relationships with introverted students can tend to be more difficult than with our extroverted students. Making a larger effort to get to know our introverted students is vital. Creating a safe environment will help give students an environment they feel comfortable in. Feeling safe helps introverts come out of their shells easier and more often (Davies, 2022).

All students love to feel valued and share their thoughts. By promoting a shared learning culture, introverts can feel as if they belong. Shared learning cultures can be created through a strong teacher-student relationship and among other students (Cain, 2016). Continuous feedback can also strengthen a relationship, making students feel loved and appreciated. One-on-one attention can help build relationships with all students, especially our introverted students. Those simple moments, such as asking a student how their morning is going or learning about what they like shows students you care about them.

By creating a safe environment, teachers can establish strong relationships. Because an introverted student will most likely not begin by volunteering information about themselves, the educator or someone working with that student will need to make a much larger effort to connect.

Relationships among peers are equally important. Creating that safe space among students requires planning and intention. Student reflection and the use of student voice can aid in this intention. This could be done between peers or teacher to student. When students are collaborating or working on a group project give them a moment to reflect, for example, by asking themselves, "What is going well with this activity? What would I change?" Students could also complete these reflections with one another, building that trust and relationship (Boroujeni et al., 2015).

Reda (2009) goes on to discuss dismantling this active-passive dichotomy, dismissing the idea that if a situation is quiet, then nothing is happening. For instance, when establishing relationships between peers or teachers and students, one might have a more active component during discussions, but respecting that the other person is learning and participating in their own unique way will build that trust needed to establish rapport and relationships among one another.

> Sometimes you can kind of create this magic with these small pockets in the classroom. . . . To me, when those things happened and we were having a real discussion and conversation about what was happening, to me, those were more magical moments, and I think more learning was happening in those moments than anything else.
>
> (Aaron)

So, how can we make these real moments of dialogue and conversation happen? Creating reflective activities as a precursor to social activities can help bridge the gap between our introverted and extroverted students (Higgins, 2017). Facilitating small-group or individual reflection can help introverts and extroverts alike. This will give students an opportunity to apply and analyze concepts, participate more fully in discussions, and solve problems. Even waiting an extra 10 seconds can give our introverts more processing time and confidence to speak (Cain, 2013a).

Introverts often prefer to listen first, so giving them time to gather their thoughts can ensure all students have a fair opportunity to participate when the time comes to have social interactions, which can be challenging. One suggestion Higgins (2017) makes is to assign roles to small groups. By having a small group role, such as a recorder, there is not as much pressure to provide oral responses within the group, but all students are still participating.

Cain (2013b) shares a think-pair strategy with a twist to increase discussion and dialogue among students. When posed with a question, instead of instantly turning and talking, students are given a moment to write or draw their thoughts. After the students have some time to write down their answers, then students turn and share with their partner. Reading from the paper is less intimidating than having to come up with a response instantaneously and share out loud at the same time.

By taking the time to create more reflection time and adapting social learning activities, such as the think/pair/share, we are giving all students an opportunity to explore and discover the learning. Students also begin to realize that even the quieter students can make large contributions to a group's responses.

When students are encouraged to explore and discover the variable skills of group members, they may come to the realization that the "quieter" member takes time to process. Students draw from one another instead of just the more extroverted students dominating these real moments.

> Some of my best moments as a teacher were working with students one-on-one or in really small groups.
>
> (Kate)

I think why this is so important for introverts is they require time to restore and gather their thoughts more often. Cain (2016) refers to this as restorative niches. These are those moments when students can return to their true selves. Working one-on-one or in very small groups gives those moments of opportunity. Cain also talked about boundaries and choice, where students could have the opportunity to "cancel a plan" if they need that time to recharge.

> One way introverts are so fundamentally different from their extroverted counterparts is that they need time alone to recharge. Spending time in large groups of people is incredibly draining for them. One way to support your introverted students is to provide them an alternative to recess. Offer a semi-quiet place – such as an open classroom – in which introverts can escape the chaos of the playground.
>
> (Green, 2017)

Introverted students can also be more responsive in small group discussions if given time to process and consider the topic. Getting acquainted and having time to warm-up or break the ice can also help all students.

You can also use the think-pair-share technique, which involves asking your students a question, asking them to think about the answer, then pairing them with another student to talk about their reflections. For introverted students, this gives them the time to process their thoughts and ensures they have the experience of expressing their thoughts out loud. Often, once they've had a run-through with another student, they're much more likely to want to share with the whole class.

Small groups can still gain whole-class perspective using a technique that Reda (2009) explains in her book *Between Speaking and Silence: A Study of Quiet Students*. When students are in small groups, the group can designate a spokesperson. When the groups disperse and the instruction returns to the whole group, each of those student spokespersons can share the small-group perspective. Why is this so important? In small groups, perspectives are limited. By sharing with the whole class, each student's perspective is honored and shared.

Sometimes I'll have a kid come to me and say, "Hey, I really don't want to present." I do allow the students who approach me to do that little presentation in front of me. Instead of standing in front of the classroom . . . Allowing students to pick and choose, it's all about their learning and not every activity has to be done independently or not every activity needs to be done as a group.

(Jill)

Since social learning activities are being promoted more than ever, by overemphasizing them, we can undermine the thinking of students who exhibit more introverted tendencies (Godsey, 2015). This can cause these students to become more easily drained through constant interaction with others. Giving students the chance to recognize where they are and make a choice as to what format they would like to present could have positive outcomes for the learning process and the student's state of mind.

Reda (2009) discussed how almost every student had a comment about her syllabus, course content, and the expectations to give presentations through public speaking format. Many students shared that in small group or one-on-one dialogue, the value of that presentation and conversation increased. The implied goals of the presentation often were not met when presented in front of many others. The comfort level to be yourself and to be free to share openly decreased. When presenting in a smaller format, genuine interaction with the participants and the teacher increased (Reda, 2009).

Fonseca, the author of *Quiet Kids* (2014), talks about the detriment of group work and collaboration if group size becomes too large or has overly extroverted group partners. When students are in groups larger than one or two additional group members, this can create an overwhelmed or frustrated response. Group sizes of two or three Fonseca describes as the ideal number. Another aspect to keep in mind is your overly extroverted group members. This can cause introverted students to shut down or contribute at a much smaller rate, inhibiting the learning for that group.

Online platforms and discussion groups for presentations could be another possible outlet for introverted students and something that all students can benefit from. With the increasing number and demand for asynchronous education, students need to start being taught how to interact in the online format (Moran, 2005).

> I have always tried to make my classroom an environment where all students felt comfortable. Where taking a risk and sharing an idea is something to be valued and celebrated. I think that is my brand of magic. To see kids as they are and help them have the courage to take a risk with their own ideas.
>
> (Sara)

As Cain herself argues, neither personality is better than the other, and each of us embodies a bit of both and can benefit from extending ourselves out of our comfort zones. Most importantly, we, both introverts and extroverts, depend on each other to do great things.

Jill during her story discussed the idea of "speed dating." Speed dating is where interactions between peers or teachers and students are kept very brief. How might this challenge students to take risks? By only expecting students to talk for, let's say, 30 seconds, students will feel more encouraged or confident with the brief expectation.

By recognizing and honoring students' unique differences and acknowledging them for who they are in their own learning journey, they will be inspired to take risks. They will know you believe in them and appreciate each effort they make to be a part of their classroom world (Stewart, 2019).

Encourage students to try new approaches to learning so they expand their repertoire of learning strategies. This doesn't have to be a 20-minute attempt to give a public speech. Thinking back to our "speed dating" example, encouraging students to take new, yet shorter, approaches will establish more confidence with the new situation or learning activity they are about to try (Dack & Tomlinson, 2015).

Kahnweiler (2018) identified challenges for introverts and the "4 Ps Process" for addressing them. Stress and people overload were two of the anxieties our introverted students and teachers might face in a school day. Prepare, presence, push, and practice were her four Ps to help introverts overcome those challenges. Within any school activity, giving students time to prepare, a supportive teacher presence, safe space to push and grow, and time to practice help introverts face those challenges and give them the tools to take risks.

References

Boroujeni, A. A., Roohani, A., & Hasanimanesh, A. (2015). The impact of extroversion and introversion personality types on EFL learners' writing ability. *Theory and Practice in Language Studies, 5*(1), 212. https://doi.org/10.17507/tpls.0501.29

Cain, S. (2013a). *Quiet: The power of introverts in a world that can't stop talking.* Broadway Paperbacks.

Cain, S. (2013b). Help shy kids – don't punish them. *The Atlantic.* www.theatlantic.com/national/archive/2013/02/help-shy-kids-dont-punish-them/273075/

Cain, S. (2016). *Quiet power: The secret strengths of introverted kids.* Puffin Books.

Dack, H., & Tomlinson, C. (2015). Inviting all students to learn. *Educational Leadership, 72*(6), 10–15.

Davies, G. (2022). How to design inclusive meetings for introverts. *Parabol.* Retrieved October 31, 2022, from www.parabol.co/blog/inclusive-meetings-introverts/

Fonseca, C. (2014). *Quiet kids: Help your introverted child succeed in an extroverted world.* Prufrock Press Inc.

Godsey, M. (2015). When schools overlook introverts. *The Atlantic.* www.theatlantic.com/education/archive/2015/09/introverts-at-school- overlook/407467

Greene, L. (2017). *How teachers can make introverts more comfortable in the classroom.* IntrovertDear.com

Higgin, T. (2017). *Five classroom strategies that help introverts and extroverts do their best work.* Common Sense Education. www.commonsense.

org/education/blog/5-classroom-strategies-that-help-introverts-and-extroverts-do-their-best-work

Houston, E. (2019). Introvert vs extrovert: A look at the spectrum & psychology. PositivePsychology.com

Kahnweiler, J. B. (2018). *The introverted leader: Building on your quiet strength*. Berrett-Koehler Publishers, Inc.

Moran, R. (2005). Enriching clinical learning experiences in community health nursing through the use of discussion boards. *International Journal of Nursing Education Scholarship*, *2*(1). https://doi.org/10.2202/1548-923x.1112

Myers, I. (2019). *Infographic: The Myers-Briggs company*. Consulting & Assessments. The Myers-Briggs Company.

Reda, M. M. (2009). *Between speaking and silence: A study of quiet students*. State University of New York Press.

Silverman, D. (1993). Beginning research. In *Interpreting qualitative data: Methods for analysing talk, text and interaction*. Sage Publications.

Stewart, J. (2019). Supporting introverted students. *BU Journal of Graduate Studies in Education*, *11*(1).

Strauss, V. (2021). Why introverts shouldn't be forced to talk in class. *The Washington Post*. www.washingtonpost.com/news/answer-sheet/wp/2013/02/12/why-introverts-shouldnt-be-forced-to-talk-in-class/

Book study guide questions

Book reflection questions for the educator

- Whose story did you connect most to and why?
- Are there other strategies you have used to connect to students who are more introverted?
- In what ways have you built relationships with other teachers that are introverted in nature?
- What is one pedagogical goal you have after reading this book?

Book reflection questions for the administrator

- ◆ Did any of these teacher stories help you to better understand your educators and students you serve?
- ◆ How can you recognize these introverted traits in your building?
- ◆ Is there a staff training or presentation you could give to build more awareness around introverts and extroverts and the power of both?
- ◆ What is one administrative goal you have after reading this book?

Conclusion – some final thoughts

Learning how to best serve our introverted students and connect with both students and teachers alike can reduce some of the anxiety and pressure we experience as educators to reach all students. *The Dead Poets Society Classroom for the Not-So-Robin Williams* will forever be the initial idea that founded this book. Each of us as teachers has this belief that we can and must create magic for our students. Through real-life, authentic teacher's stories and experiences and the amazing research that has been done around introverts, even the not-so-extroverted educator can find success and what works for them. Not all classroom magic is the same.

Education is a stressful world today. All of the increasing demands that we as teachers (and students) have every day that we enter the classroom continues to grow. Engaging students, creating magic in your classroom, and finding opportunities for all students to be successful are demands we feel every day. Knowing that all students are not the same can add further stress and pressure to create an environment where every student can be successful.

Probably the most fascinating part of this entire book journey has been that even though each teacher's story was unique and incredible in its own way, there were many commonalities among them. Small and intimate settings, relationships, choice, and participation were themes that ran deep amongst all six of the teachers' stories.

Creating small and intimate atmospheres is something that all students can thrive in. Our introverted students survive and grow in these settings. One-on-one conversations, small groups, and teacher and student discussions, all aid in these students (and teachers) being successful.

Relationships – this is a golden ticket for all teachers and students. Even more important is to establish the trust needed for introverts to feel comfortable sharing and working with others. Relationships need to be solid for introverts to thrive.

Choice and participation are valuable tools for all students. But for introverts, this can help minimize fear, lack of participation, and the feeling of survival mode that they can feel when placed in certain situations or assignments. The simple choice of how to participate, how to present information, or whether to work alone or with a partner are all the more important.

Thank you for taking this journey with me through the lives of six real, introverted, yet dynamic, teachers. As the Dalai Lama once said, "Silence is sometimes the best answer."

Printed in the United States
by Baker & Taylor Publisher Services